Beyond the Garden Gate

THOMAS KINKADE

HARVEST HOUSE PUBLISHERS
Eugene, Oregon 97402

BEYOND THE GARDEN GATE

He has

made

everything

beautiful

in its

time.

~ THE BOOK OF ECCLESIASTES

When at last I took the time

to look into the heart of a flower,

it opened up a whole new world —

a world where every country walk

would be an adventure,

where every garden would become

an enchanted one.

~ PRINCESS GRACE OF MONACO

When the sun declined

toward the west afternoon,

I sat in the shade and from the veranda

turned the hose with its fine sprinkler

all over the garden. Oh, the joy of it!

The delicious scents from earth and leaves,

the glitter of drops on the young green,

the gratitude of all the plants

at the refreshing bath

and draught of water!

~ CELIA THAXTER

He strayed down a walk edged with box;
with apple trees, pear trees,
and cherry trees on one side,
and a border on the other,
full of all sorts of old-fashioned flowers,
stocks, sweet-williams, primroses,
pansies, mingled with southern-wood,
sweet-briar, and various fragrant herbs.
They were fresh now as a succession
of April showers and gleams,
followed by a lovely spring morning,
could make them: the sun was just
entering the dappled east,
and his light illumined the wreathed
and dewy orchard trees and shone down
the quiet walks under them.

"Jane, will you have a flower?"

~ CHARLOTTE BRONTË
JANE EYRE

The sun shone down for nearly a week on the secret garden.

The Secret Garden was what Mary called it

when she was thinking of it. She liked the name,

and she liked still more the feeling that when its

beautiful old walls shut her in no one knew where she was.

It seemed almost like being shut out

of the world in some fairy place....

The bulbs in the secret garden

must have been much astonished.

Such nice clear places were made round them that

they had all the breathing space they wanted, and really,

if Mistress Mary had known it, they began to cheer up

under the dark earth and work tremendously.

The sun could get at them and warm them,

and when the rain came down

it could reach them at once,

so they began to feel very much alive.

~ FRANCES HODGSON BURNETT
THE SECRET GARDEN

verywhere the lanes

were fragrant with wild roses,

and honeysuckle and

the breeze came to us

over the hedges laden

with the perfume

of the clover-fields

and grass-meadows.

~ EDITH HOLDEN

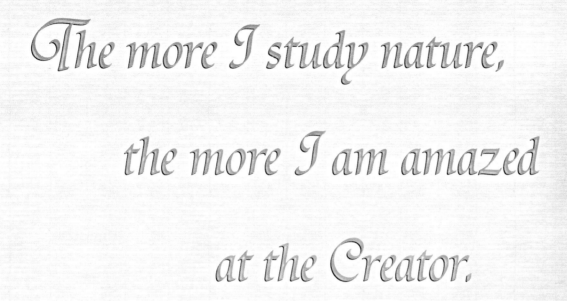

The more I study nature,

the more I am amazed

at the Creator.

~ LOUIS PASTEUR

Close to the gates a spacious garden lies,

From storms defended, and inclement skies:

Four acres was the allotted space of ground,

Fenced with a green enclosure all around.

Tall thriving trees confessed the fruitful mould;

The reddening apple ripens here to gold,

Here the blue fig with luscious juice o'erflows,

With deeper red the full pomegranate glows,

Then branch here bends beneath the weighty pear,

And verdant olives flourish round the year.

The balmy spirit of the western gale

Eternal breathes on fruits untaught to fail;

Each dropping pear a following pear supplies,

On apples apples, figs on figs arise:

The same mild season gives the blooms to blow,

The buds to harden, and the fruits to grow.

~ HOMER

*U*nder and among the groups

of leafless oaks and beeches

were blue hepaticas, white anemones,

violets and celandines in sheets.

The celandines in particular

delighted me with their clean,

happy brightness, so beautifully

trim and newly varnished,

as though they too had had

the painters at work on them.

I felt so absolutely happy and blest,

and thankful, and grateful,

that I really cannot describe it.

My days seemed to melt away

in a dream of pink and purple peace.

~ ELIZABETH AND HER GERMAN GARDEN

There come to me a few glad moments, when
    The busy day is ended, and I stray
Into the garden, shut away from men
    And all their tasks and all the sports they play.

The birds are homing for the coming night,
    The air is still and peaceful and serene,
But there's a beauty in the fading light
    Which at the noon of day is seldom seen.

Pansies and poppies, peonies and phlox,
    All with a long day's toil complete to view!
Trees which have stood perennial storms and shocks,
    Old as the world, yet always young and new.

I walk among them where the shadows fall,
    And seem to feel in touch with things divine;
Who knows, but I am brother to them all,
    Brother to bluebell, rose and columbine?

~ EDGAR A. GUEST

*T*hen, wriggling our toes in the mud

like eight-year-olds,

we closed the garden gate,

wiped our feet on the lawn grass,

lifted our faces, eyes shut,

mouths wide, drank the rain as it fell,

and were one with grass and trees.

~ HAL BORLAND

One touch
of nature
makes
the whole
world
kin.

or is the fragrant garden

ever wholly our own....

Over hedge or wall,

and often far down the highway,

it sends a greeting,

not alone to us

who have toiled for it,

but to the passing stranger,

the blind beggar,

the child skipping to school,

the tired woman on her way to work,

the rich man,

the careless youth.

~ LOUISE BEEBE WILDER

I knew by the smoke that so gracefully curled

Above the green elms, that a cottage was near.

And I said, if there's peace to be found in the world,

A heart that was humble might hope for it here.

~ THOMAS MOORE

All the seasons

run their

race

In this quiet

resting

place...

~ Austin Dobson

he fine old place never looked

more like a delightful home

than at that moment:

the great white lilies were in flower;

the nasturtiums,

their pretty leaves all silvered with dew,

were running away over the low stone wall;

the very noises all around

had a heart of peace

within them.

~ GEORGE ELIOT

So then the year is repeating its old story again.

We are come once more, thank God!

to its most charming chapter.

The violets and the May flowers

are as its inscriptions or vignettes.

It always makes a pleasant

impression on us,

when we open again

at these pages of

the book of life.

~ Johann Wolfgang von Goethe

*G*od is in me

as the sun

is in the

fragrance

and color

of a flower.

~ HELEN KELLER

Every rose

is an

autograph

from

the hand

of God.

~ Theodore Parker

 h, I could dance and sing for joy that spring is here!

What a resurrection of beauty there is in my garden,

and of brightest hope in my heart!

The whole of this radiant Easter day I have spent out of doors,

sitting at first among the windflowers and celandines,

and then later, walking in the green paths,

my heart full of happiest gratitude.

It makes one very humble to see one-self surrounded

by such a wealth of beauty and perfection anonymously lavished.

I do sincerely trust that the benediction that is always

awaiting me in my garden may by degrees be more deserved,

and that I may grow in grace and patience, and cheerfulness,

just like the happy flowers I so much love.

~ ELIZABETH AND HER GERMAN GARDEN

The morning dawns with an unwonted crimson;

the flowers more odorous seem;

the garden birds sing louder,

and the laughing sun

ascends the gaudy earth

with an unusual brightness:

all nature smiles,

and the whole world is pleased.

~ Day Kellogg Lee

I pushed the gate that swings so silently,

And I was in the garden and aware

Of early daylight on the flowers there

And cups of dew sun-kindled.

~ PAUL VERLAINE

Let the heavens rejoice,

and let the earth be glad....

Let the field be joyful

and all that is therein:

then shall all

the trees

of the wood

rejoice.

~ THE BOOK OF PSALMS

Paintings

Glory of Morning
Gardens Beyond Autumn Gate
Home Is Where the Heart Is II
Lilac Gazebo
The Hidden Cottage

Spring at Stonegate
Morning Dogwood
Meadowood Cottage
Spring Gate
Garden of Promise
Merritt's Cottage
Glory of Evening
Hidden Cottage II

Julianne's Cottage
Beside Still Waters
Chandler's Cottage
Rose Gate
The Hidden Gazebo
Brookside Hideaway
The Victorian Garden
Petals of Hope